STUDY GUIDE

WHEN YOU'VE BEEN WRONGED

MOVING FROM BITTERNESS TO FORGIVENESS

ERWIN W. LUTZER

MOODY PUBLISHERS
CHICAGO

D0110515

All Scripture quotations, unless otherwise indicated, are taken from *The Holy Bible, English Standard Version.* Copyright © 2000, 2001 by Crossway Bibles, a division of Good News Publishers. Used by permission. All rights reserved.

Developed by Sam O'Neal
Interior design: Ragont Design
Cover design: Kirk DuPonce / Dog Eared Design; Kathryn Joachim

ISBN-13: 978-0-8024-8899-2

We hope you enjoy this book from Moody Publishers. Our goal is to provide high-quality, thought-provoking books and products that connect truth to your real needs and challenges. For more information on other books and products written and produced from a biblical perspective, go to www. moodypublishers.com or write to:

Moody Publishers
820 N. LaSalle Boulevard
Chicago, IL 60610

3 5 7 9 10 8 6 4

Printed in the United States of America

CONTENTS

INTRODUCTION

THIS STUDY GUIDE is to be used with the book and DVD series, both of which are titled *When You've Been Wronged* by Dr. Erwin Lutzer (available from Moody Publishers).

This guide is intended for both the group leader and also for the participants who wish to read the relevant sections of the book and respond to the DVD presentations.

Although the content of the book and the DVD series are essentially the same, there are some differences in the order the material is presented. For this reason, each set of study questions begins by giving specific information as to what parts of the book should be read in preparation for the DVD lecture and the questions to follow.

Simply read the section in the *When You've Been Wronged* book that is labeled **please read**, and you will be prepared for both the lecture and the questions below.

DVD Session One

WHEN YOU RECEIVE AN OFFENSE

In preparation for these discussion questions
and the DVD lecture, **please read:**
Chapter 1, "Satan's Mixed Bag of Offenses"
Chapter 2, "The Blinding Power of an Offense"

From the Author

WHEN AN OFFENSE festers in our hearts, we cannot confine it within our souls. Instead, it spills over in ways we don't even realize. It's like burning incense in a dormitory. The smell cannot be confined; rather it escapes the dorm room and wafts down the hallway, into the washrooms, and all the way to the front door.

Just so, our bitterness spills over into other relationships no matter how determined we are to keep it confined to a single room within our soul. Nursing an offense quite literally blinds us to our own faults, forces us to have skewed relationships, and warps our self-perceptions.

Ultimately, the path to healing is to follow Christ's example.

"When they hurled their insults at him, he did not retaliate; when he suffered, he made no threats. Instead, he entrusted himself to him who judges justly" (1 Peter 2:23). This may be a worn-out cliché but it's true: you have to give it to God.

ENGAGING THE TOPIC

Answer these questions while watching the DVD and reading the book.

1. An _____ is a stumbling block, something that is thrown into your life and keeps you from following God.

2. _____, unless they are given up, never leave our souls.

3. A person who maintains an offense lives within a wall of _____.

4. Those who maintain bitterness become blind to their own _____.

5. Whatever you don't _____ you pass on.

6. A person who maintains an offense frequently seeks _____.

7. A person who maintains an offense can become a _____.

8. A person who hangs on to an offense succumbs to _____.

OPENING ACTIVITY

Purpose: To help the group think about the pervasiveness of a festering offense.

Supplies: A bag of microwave popcorn; a microwave.

Activity: Tell the group you'll be cooking some popcorn, but they must keep themselves from smelling it. There are only two rules: no one may leave the room while the popcorn is popping, and no one may turn off the microwave. Otherwise, they can take any measure they can think of to keep from smelling the popcorn.

Alternate: Coffee, incense, or a strong scented candle can be used if popcorn is not available.

QUESTIONS FOR DISCUSSION

1. What moments of betrayal do you recall most vividly from books, movies, and television shows? Why did those scenes make an impact on you?

2. List the five types of offenses Satan uses to keep us bound.

3. Read Proverbs 18:19. How have you seen this principle illustrated in your life and relationships?

4. Read 1 John 2:9–11. What are some ways this kind of hate manifests itself in our Western culture? What are some ways this kind of hate manifests itself in our church culture?

5. Discuss the idea of vengeance. Is it ever appropriate for followers of God to avenge themselves after an attack or an offense? Why or why not?

6. Read Ezekiel 14:1–5. How is refusing to let go of bitterness equivalent to idolatry?

7. What benefits do we receive by holding on to offenses and bitterness? Why do we do it?

8. If you are willing to discuss them, what moments of betrayal do you recall most vividly from your past? Have you let go of those offenses, or are you still holding on to the bitterness they caused?

GOING DEEPER

Read Psalm 55 out loud.

1. Discuss the emotions specifically mentioned by the author, as well as the imagery he uses. How do you react to them?

2. Notice the requests the author gives to God (verses 1–2, 9). Are these appropriate for a follower of God?

3. What event caused David to write this psalm? (See verses 12–15.) How does this foreshadow the experiences of Jesus (a descendant of David)?

4. What is the turning point of this psalm—what verse shows David's posture and emotions moving in a different direction? What direction is he moving to?

5. How would you summarize David's conclusions at the end of this psalm? (See verses 22–23.) What would it take for you to say and feel something similar?

Personal Reflection

It's one of Jesus' most frightening proclamations: "You have heard that it was said to those of old, 'You shall not murder; and whoever murders will be liable to judgment.' But I say to you that everyone who is angry with his brother will be liable to judgment; whoever insults his brother will be liable to the council; and whoever says, 'You fool!' will be liable to the hell of fire" (Matthew 5:21–22).

On one hand, we know that Jesus' words are true because we have been wounded by the words and actions of others. We have felt the brunt of our brother's anger and the sting of our brother's insults. We have been betrayed. We bear the scars of broken promises, broken confidences, rejection, false accusations, and abuse.

On the other hand, we know that Jesus' words are true because we have taken aim with words and actions of our own. We have unleashed our anger on our brother; we have cried "You fool!" We have betrayed. We have delivered broken promises, broken confidences, rejection, false accusations, and abuse.

The result is an ever-increasing cycle of offenses given and offenses received, with no end in sight to be achieved through our own resources.

Do you have the courage to turn to Jesus and break free?

Engaging the Topic answers:
1. offense 2. Offenses 3. bitterness 4. faults 5. forgive 6. vengeance 7. destroyer 8. idolatry

WHEN YOU ENCOUNTER A DESTROYER

In preparation for these discussion questions
and the DVD lecture, **please read:**
Chapter 3, "Meet Cain the Destroyer"

From the Author

THE FIRST OFFSPRING in this world was Cain: "Adam lay with his wife Eve, and she became pregnant and gave birth to Cain" (Genesis 4:1). Adam and Eve were the first parents to raise a Cain, but they were not the last. Cain represents those individuals I call *destroyers;* the kind of people who can leave you bleeding along the road and walk away feeling sorry for themselves.

Destroyers are found everywhere: they are found in Christian homes, in churches, and at the office. Most surprising, some are charming, helpful, and delightfully pleasant. But when they have an opportunity—particularly if they feel that their image or authority is attacked—they will destroy anyone who stands in their path. They are obsessed with self-protection and will manipulate, threaten, and distort; yet they feel no guilt. They believe the entire world should stoop to serve them, and they let everyone know why.

A destroyer is the kind of person for whom appearances are everything. Manipulative, ruthless, insidious, and murderous, he will work against you, lie to your face, and chisel away at your emotional core until you are totally diminished spiritually, emotionally, and at times, physically. Destroying others guarantees his sense of self-worth. A destroyer can hurt you deeply yet feel no sympathy. A destroyer is actually incapable of feeling hurt for anybody else, yet is keenly aware of the emotional pain he himself carries.

ENGAGING THE TOPIC

Answer these questions while watching the DVD and reading the book.

1. A _____ will leave you wounded and walk away feeling sorry for himself.

2. For every _____ that exists there is a _____ who did it.

3. The first characteristic of Cain is that he refuses _____.

4. The second characteristic of Cain is that he refuses _____ for his sin.

5. The third characteristic of Cain is that he is _____.

6. Either we will _____ sin or sin will _____ us.

7. We must be _____ by the _____ that forgives us.

OPENING ACTIVITY

Purpose: To provide a personal entry point for Cain's story.

Supplies: A sheet of paper and pen/pencil for each group member.

Activity: Have someone read aloud Cain's story from Genesis 4:8–16. After the story has been read, have the group members each make a list of people who have hurt or retaliated against them in a painful way. They might also include occasions where they have hurt or retaliated against someone else. When everyone is finished writing, have them tuck their lists into their Bibles for consideration after the session is finished.

QUESTIONS FOR DISCUSSION

1. Dr. Lutzer paints a bleak picture of the nature of destroyers: "Manipulative, ruthless, insidious, and murderous, he will work against you, lie to your face, and chisel away at your emotional core until you are totally diminished spiritually, emotionally, and at times, physically." Do such people exist in your life?

2. Read Genesis 4:1–7. What emotions do you typically experience when God does not react how you expect (or desire) Him to?

3. Discuss God's command to "rule over" sin. How could Cain have accomplished this? How can we accomplish this today?

4. Drawing on information from the book and the lecture, list some of the ways people can identify a destroyer.

5. Read Genesis 4:8–16. Looking specifically at verse 10, summarize why the words "to me" are vitally important.

6. Read Genesis 3:14–24, and reread Genesis 4:11–12. What do these two passages say about the nature and consequences of sin?

7. In your opinion, what is our culture's conventional wisdom when it comes to dealing with destroyers?

8. How would you summarize the wisdom of God's Word when it comes to dealing with destroyers?

GOING DEEPER

Read 1 John 3:1–18.

1. Discuss the significance of verse 2. What does it mean that "we are God's children now"?

2. Summarize the view of sin given in verses 4–10. Do Christians forfeit their relationship with God when they sin?

3. Why is Cain described as being "of the evil one," yet Adam and Eve are not?

4. Read Matthew 5:21–22. How does this contribute to your understanding of the passage in 1 John? How does it contribute to your understanding of Cain's story?

5. What do the author's statements in verses 16–18 mean for Christians today? How can we obey?

PERSONAL REFLECTION

The apostle Peter wrote what may be the most-feared warning of the New Testament: "Be sober-minded; be watchful. Your adversary the devil prowls around like a roaring lion, seeking someone to devour" (1 Peter 5:8).

Most Christians don't need much persuading when it comes to heeding this warning. We want to "be watchful," because we have been taught that the enemy is indeed out there somewhere. The devil is real, and he has real power to cause us pain. He is not just lurking in the shadows but prowling. He is actively looking for us, and he wants to bring us down.

Upon further reflection, however, God's warning to Cain is more terrifying still: "If you do not do well, sin is crouching at the door. Its desire is for you, but you must rule over it" (Genesis 4:7b). This is another enemy entirely: our own sinful nature. All of a sudden the danger is not "out there" somewhere, trying to find us. Rather, it is inside of us; it is part of us. We are the enemy, and we have power not only to harm ourselves but others. Like Cain, we can become destroyers if we do not "rule over" our sin.

Two enemies—both of them real, and both of them dangerous. And yet both of them conquered by the blood of Jesus Christ. His sacrifice "speaks a better word than the blood of Abel" (Hebrews 10:24) because it offers forgiveness and reconciliation, rather than judgment.

Will you accept this forgiveness? And if you have already accepted it, will you commit this week to exploring the areas of your life that are in need of reconciliation?

Engaging the Topic answers:

1. destroyer 2. hurt; hurter 3. counsel 4. responsibility 5. self-absorbed
6. master; master 7. reconciled; blood

WHEN FAMILY MEMBERS FIGHT

In preparation for these discussion questions
and the DVD lecture, **please read:**
Chapter 4, "Families at War: When Trust Fails"

From the Author

THE FAMILY IS the crucible in which the most intimate
and potentially devastating relationships occur. It is the envi-
ronment in which we learn our identity and our self-worth—
it is there we find ultimate acceptance, emotional care, and
nurturing. But because so much is riding on the family, it has
also become the place of enormous conflict. Nowhere is reconciliation more needed and nowhere is it more difficult to attain.

Jealousy, I suspect, has torn apart more family relationships than any other single factor. As a pastor, I've witnessed
it more times than I can count. And by the time the frac-
tured families come to me, the damage often is deep, and the

prognosis for recovery bleak. Inheritance and money can cause deep rifts in families too.

Thankfully, God desires to bring healing. The Bible helps us with real-life examples of His provision during times of family pain. Perhaps the most compelling story about family strife is the story of Jacob and Esau. What sparks flew in that home! Still, God in His goodness came through with unexpected peace and healing. In the process of taking a look at this family feud, we shall learn some lessons about how to initiate forgiveness and reconciliation. We shall also discover that God is often gracious even to a dysfunctional family.

ENGAGING THE TOPIC

Answer these questions while watching the DVD and reading the book.

1. The first huge problem in this family is _____.

2. We also see _____ on the part of Jacob.

3. There is _____ in this family, and it is huge.

4. In our families today we need _____.

5. God is at work in _____ families.

6. It is necessary for family systems to have _____ in order to _____ each other.

OPENING ACTIVITY

Purpose: To help the group think about blessings within families.

Supplies: A sheet of paper and pen/pencil for each group member.

Activity: Have each group member write a blessing for someone within his or her extended family. The blessing can either be written for another member of the family, or it can express a blessing you would like to hear *from* a member of the family. When everyone has finished, have group members:

- Read their blessings if they are comfortable doing so.
- Describe blessings that were well done. These might be from personal experience or picked up from friends, film, literature, and so on.

QUESTIONS FOR DISCUSSION

1. What one word best described your family during your childhood?

2. Read Genesis 25:19–28. What other families in the Bible suffered negative consequences because of favoritism?

3. Read Genesis 25:29–34. In your opinion, which of the brothers was at fault? Which one made the worst decision?

4. Discuss the idea of sacrificing the permanent on the altar of the immediate. Where else does this mind-set occur in the Bible? Where do you find this mind-set in today's culture?

5. Read Genesis 27:1–40. What is Rebekah's motivation for instigating this scheme? What other characters in Scripture make decisions based on a similar motivation?

6. As a result of Rebekah's plot, God's prophetic words from Genesis 25:23 were fulfilled. Does this justify her decision? Why do you say so?

7. Discuss the blessing Isaac delivers in 27:27–29. What stands out to you as most interesting? Do you find anything to be surprising or confusing?

8. Read Genesis 27:41–45. In your opinion, are conflicts within a family easier or more difficult to resolve than conflicts outside of a family? Explain your answer.

GOING DEEPER

Read Genesis 31:17–55.

1. What was the primary source of the conflict in these events?

2. What was Laban's motivation in pursuing Jacob and his family? Did he achieve what he set out to accomplish?

3. What do we learn from Rachel's actions in this scene? Where did she learn to lie and deceive?

4. Verses 36–50 offer emotional speeches from both Jacob and Laban. In your experience, what is the benefit of "laying everything out on the table"? What were the results in this scene?

5. Did reconciliation occur between Jacob and Laban? Between their families?

PERSONAL REFLECTION

In Exodus 34:7, God tells Moses that He is active in "visiting the iniquity of the fathers on the children and the children's children, to the third and the fourth generation." Bible scholars and theologians debate how literally we should interpret this statement. But there is no debate about the general principle behind these words of God. Namely, that poor decisions made by parents often impact their children (and their children's children) in negative ways. Moreover, a parent's poor decisions are often repeated by his or her progeny. These truths are illustrated multiple times throughout the book of Genesis alone.

In Genesis 12, for example, we see Abraham claim that his wife, Sarah, was actually his sister in order to save himself from harm. The worst possible consequences are averted through the intervention of God, but we see Isaac, Abraham's son, attempt the same deception in Genesis 26. Then there is the familial favoritism demonstrated by Isaac and Rebekah in Genesis 25. Jacob and Esau were separated for decades as a result of this favoritism, and yet that did not stop Jacob from blatantly favoring Joseph over his other sons (see Genesis 37 and following).

Generational sin is a phenomenon with real and damaging consequences. This is a sobering thought, and it raises an important question: How will the decisions you make today affect the members of your family (and their subsequent families) in the years to come? What changes are you willing to make now in order to save your children and your children's children from future harm?

Engaging the Topic answers:
1. favoritism 2. jealousy 3. deception 4. boundaries 5. dysfunctional
6. boundaries; understand

WHEN YOU WANT TO RECONCILE

In preparation for these discussion questions
and the DVD lecture, **please read:**
Chapter 4, "Families at War: When Trust Fails" (pages 64–74)
Chapter 8, "The High Cost of Reconciliation"

From the Author

THE QUESTION OFTEN raised in connection with reconciliation is: Why bother? After all, when you try to restore a relationship, you might be met with misunderstanding or outright rejection. Here are four reasons why Christians should attempt to restore broken relationships among families and among believers.

First, reconciliation must be attempted because of our witness to the world. The mark of the Christian, according to Francis Schaeffer, is *love*—love for one another. That's how we are known to the world—or should be. When we can't get along as Christians, it invalidates our faith.

Second, Christians pursue reconciliation in order to

influence future generations. Sadly, Christian families, just like non-Christian families, can be consumed and divided by conflict. The ongoing feud between the Hatfields and the McCoys can serve as a humorous but painful metaphor for the way many Christian families operate today. Remember, what we don't forgive, we pass on. As parents, we should model love and forgiveness before our children, passing on those qualities to the next generation.

Third, without reconciliation, there is disunity, which weakens the body of Jesus Christ. This is why racial reconciliation is so crucial for our Christian life and witness. If we are divided over race, we prove to the world that our bond in Christ is not very strong—at least not as strong as the color of our skin or ethnic background. Nor can a family stand that's divided against itself—father against mother, child against parent (see Mark 3:25). It rips, it tears, it hurts, and it weakens the body of Christ every time.

Finally, reconciled Christians demonstrate the power of Christ's gospel.

ENGAGING THE TOPIC

Answer these questions while watching the DVD and reading the book.

1. _____ is the initiator of reconciliation.

2. Jacob uses an expression of _____ to prepare the way for reconciliation with Esau.

3. Jacob seeks _____ to prepare for reconciliation.

4. God _____ Jacob so all his dependence will be complete.

5. God uses a _____ _____ to make a straight line.

6. Reconciliation is indeed _____ work.

7. You cannot have full reconciliation without _____, _____, and _____.

OPENING ACTIVITY

Purpose: To appreciate the setting for Jacob's struggle.
Supplies: A good memory.
Activity: Relate to the group as many unlikely matchups as you can remember. These might be personal experiences, scenes from film or literature, fables, or even head-to-heads you'd like to see. In each case, discuss what was at stake and how the uneven matches turned out.

QUESTIONS FOR DISCUSSION

1. How would you define reconciliation in your own words?

2. Divide the group into smaller clusters (two or three people in each), and assign one of the following Scripture passages to each subgroup. Allow five minutes for the subgroups to read and discuss their

passage, then ask each to answer this question: How does your passage contribute to our understanding of reconciliation?

- Matthew 5:23–24
- James 4:10
- 2 Corinthians 5:18–20
- Matthew 6:14–15
- 1 Peter 5:6

3. Read Genesis 32:3–21. Which of Jacob's actions in this passage are positive? Which do you believe are negative, if any? Explain.

4. Read Genesis 32:22–31. What is the significance of God changing Jacob's name to Israel? (Refer back to 25:26 for additional information.)

5. In what ways do people wrestle with God today? Have you struggled with God over the desire for a blessing?

6. Read Genesis 33:1–17. Which of Jacob's actions in this passage are positive? Which do you believe are negative, if any?

7. In chapter 8 of his book, Dr. Lutzer suggests "Six Steps to Genuine Reconciliation" (see pages 138–46). How many of these steps does Jacob follow in his reconnection with Esau?

8. Are you currently experiencing relationships that are damaged and in need of reconciliation? For those willing to share, what is the next step you need to take along that road?

Going Deeper

Take a deeper look at Genesis 33:1–20.

1. How would you characterize Jacob's attitude toward his brother throughout this chapter? Why does Jacob feel this way?

2. How would you characterize Esau's attitude toward his brother throughout this chapter? Has it been your experience that "time heals all wounds"?

3. Discuss the significance of Jacob offering a "blessing" to Esau (see verse 11). What does Jacob's attempt to repair the wrong he committed show about his desire for reconciliation?

4. Does reconciliation occur between Jacob and Esau? Why or why not?

PERSONAL REFLECTION

Christians can sometimes view forgiveness and reconciliation as "feel-good" practices, calling to mind movie climaxes where formerly bitter characters throw aside their anger in favor of a slow-motion hug.

Yet many of Jesus' thoughts on those subjects are more sobering. For example: "For if you forgive men when they sin against you, your heavenly Father will also forgive you. But if you do not forgive men their sins, your Father will not forgive your sins" (Matthew 6:14–15). The principle here is that a refusal to forgive will ultimately produce self-inflicted wounds —and may damage our relationship with God.

And consider this one: "If you are offering your gift at the altar and there remember that your brother has something against you, leave your gift . . . go and be reconciled to your brother; then come and offer your gift" (Matthew 5:23–24). Again, there is a connection between reconciliation in our earthly relationships and the quality of our relationship with our heavenly Father.

If that gives you pause or makes you feel worried, you are not alone. But the good news is that you can do something about it.

Engaging the Topic answers:
1. God 2. goodwill 3. God 4. weakens 5. crooked stick 6. God's
7. forgiveness; trust; respect

DVD Session Five

WHEN YOU'RE UNDER ATTACK

In preparation for these discussion questions
and the DVD lecture, **please read**:
Chapter 5, "Dodging Spears"

From the Author

BULLIES HURT—and their words and attacks can stay with you for a lifetime. The old saw about bullies can be revised: "Sticks and stones will break my bones, and names will always harm me."

But there are adult bullies too. These are not physically intimidating people, sporting strange horns or wearing angry scowls on their faces. Yet they operate in offices and churches, and you might find some among your relatives. Some of you who are reading these words are married to one.

These adult bullies might more accurately be labeled *spear throwers*. They are those individuals hell-bent on damaging and threatening you—even destroying you or your reputation.

Motivated by jealousy, they stop at nothing to make certain you melt into a pool of fear and shame at their words or actions.

Spear throwers like to make people squirm. They are self-absorbed, self-motivated, and self-deceived. And they do it all cloaked with verses of Scripture and hidden behind the loftiest motives. These people exist in offices, in neighborhoods, and sometimes within our own homes. Many of them claim a deep relationship with God. They may be Sunday school teachers, social workers, and devoted parents. Amazingly, they can be caring and thoughtful—and mean and evil—all at once.

A discussion on the subject of overcoming wrongs would be incomplete without addressing the topic of spear throwers and how to deal with them from God's perspective.

Engaging the Topic

Answer these questions while watching the DVD and reading the book.

1. A _____ _____ is someone who enjoys hurting other people or likes to assert their authority.

2. The first characteristic of Saul was that he was _____ by God.

3. The second characteristic of Saul was that he had the _____ gift.

4. The third characteristic of Saul was that he had military _____ and _____.

5. Saul had a sense of _____. He believed the
   _____ was his and not God's.

OPENING ACTIVITY

Purpose: To introduce the theme of spear throwing in our own context.

Supplies: Something of value, whether a gift card, $20 bill, or whatever would represent value in your group.

Activity: Talk about the gift in as favorable a light as possible. Play up its value. Then decide on a method to award it to someone. Either the leader picks arbitrarily, you have a contest, you draw straws, vote, or flip a coin. Did the exercise create a spark of jealousy in anyone? Anyone sense feelings that the outcome was wrong or unfair? If not, discuss examples of life situations that *have* provoked jealousy in the group. Based on the intensity of the emotion (e.g., in a close relationship), what are some possible strong reactions you could actually picture stemming from such jealousy?

QUESTIONS FOR DISCUSSION

1. Dr. Lutzer describes spear throwers as "impossible people" in the video lecture. In your opinion, is it possible for someone to be a spear thrower and a follower of Jesus at the same time?

2. Read 1 Samuel 10:1, 9–11. Discuss the phrase "God gave him another heart" (verse 9). How do you understand that phrase given what you know of Saul's later behavior as a "spear thrower"?

3. What are other examples from Scripture of leaders who started out well but ultimately faltered?

4. Read 1 Samuel 15:22–31. Which of Saul's actions were positive? Which actions revealed a sinful heart?

5. What attitudes, desires, or circumstances commonly prevent Christians today from obeying God's commands?

6. Read 1 Samuel 18:6–16. Discuss the phrase "a harmful spirit from God rushed upon Saul." Was Saul responsible for his actions as a spear thrower, or was God?

7. God is sometimes referred to as "jealous" in Scripture (e.g., Exodus 34:13–14). What is the difference between the jealousy of God and the jealously demonstrated by people?

8. How should Christians today react to spear throwers who are followers of Jesus? How should Christians react to spear throwers who do not follow Jesus?

GOING DEEPER

Read 1 Samuel 19:1–24.

1. What do you learn about Saul's character in these verses? Jonathan's? David's?

2. Read verse 9 again. Why is it significant that the author stresses Saul "sat in his house with his spear in hand"?

3. What was David's best defense against Saul's consistent attacks? Are you able to rely on friends and family for support against the spear throwers in your life?

4. How would you summarize verses 18–24? What is the primary lesson we can learn from those verses?

PERSONAL REFLECTION

When it comes to the different men and women profiled throughout the pages of the Bible, Saul is among the least popular—and with good reason. After all, he deliberately disobeyed a prophet of God and then comically attempted to deny it. He sent a boy to fight a giant in his place. He used his own daughter as a pawn in political manipulations. He relentlessly pursued an innocent man who had served him well for many years.

Yes, Saul made a lot of bad decisions, and therefore he deserves much blame. But that is why David's actions in 1 Samuel 24 are so interesting. To set the scene, while Saul and his army were hunting David in an effort to kill him, David found Saul alone in a cave:

> And afterward David's heart struck him, because he had cut off a corner of Saul's robe. He said to his men, "The Lord forbid that I should do this thing to my lord, the Lord's anointed, to put out my hand against him, seeing he is the Lord's anointed." So David persuaded his men with these words and did not permit them to attack Saul. And Saul rose up and left the cave and went on his way. (1 Samuel 24:5–7)

David later goes so far as to humble himself in front of the king, even bowing down and paying homage. He says: "After whom has the king of Israel come out? After whom do you pursue? After a dead dog! After a flea! May the Lord therefore be judge and give sentence between me and you, and see to it and plead my cause and deliver me from your hand" (1 Samuel 24:14–15).

As you listen to Dr. Lutzer speak about spear throwers, it may be easy to form a picture in your mind of people you know that fit the description. Like David, you may have a major spear thrower in your life who is causing you great pain. But remember that David chose to allow God to determine justice in the areas he had been wronged.

Will you?

Engaging the Topic answers:

1. spear thrower 2. anointed 3. prophetic 4. victories; ability

5. entitlement; kingdom

WHEN
YOU WANT
TO SUE

In preparation for these discussion questions
and the DVD lecture, **please read:**
Chapter 5, "Dodging Spears" (pages 87–95)
Chapter 6, "Christians in the Courtroom"

From the Author

WHY IS AMERICA such a litigious nation? There's a simple answer—but one with complex implications. We are living in a culture that exalts individual rights even as it accepts a decline (and corruption) of personal morals and integrity. Put the two together and you have a recipe for rampant lawsuits.

Remember the news account—yes, it's a true story—of two sets of parents who went to court after their children, playing in a sandbox, got into a big argument? It used to be that parents could work those things out, when character was important. But today without character they cannot even settle such minor matters. Today we need a law for everything, and God help us if we don't receive what we believe to be our individual "rights."

Indeed, America has seen an alarming decrease in individual responsibility and a heightened insistence on one's personal rights in the last fifty to sixty years. And unfortunately, God's Word notwithstanding, Christians have absorbed the culture and are suing one another.

The Bible clearly outlines the involvement of Christians in the courtroom. As we will see, when we seek our own justice when personal injury occurs, we ignore our need to forgive, as well as God's ability to obtain eventual justice. To better understand our response and God's, we need to look at what the Bible says about legal action among and by believers after an offense.

ENGAGING THE TOPIC

Answer these questions while watching the DVD and reading the book.

1. Try, if you can, to _____ the spear.

2. A truly evil person sees the _____ that is in him as residing in other people.

3. Don't even try to _____ with a spear thrower.

4. Don't become a _____ in return.

5. When it comes to spear throwers, we have to let _____ deal with them.

6. Learn the _____ God wants to _____ us.

7. God wants to chip away everything in our lives that isn't _____, and He will even use _____ people to do it.

OPENING ACTIVITY

Purpose: To help group members assess our culture's view of courtrooms and lawsuits.

Supplies: A list of books, films, or personal examples of "legal thriller" stories to prime the pump for group discussion.

Activity: Have group members recount what they remember of the "legal thriller" stories they've seen or read—or give personal examples of lawsuits or legal entanglements. If you have copies of such books on hand (e.g., John Grisham), someone can read the promotional copy on the back covers. When all of the stories have been told, discuss:

- Which story sounded the most interesting to you? Why?
- What themes were shared by the stories?
- What do these stories reveal about how we view courtrooms and the legal profession?

QUESTIONS FOR DISCUSSION

1. Discuss Dr. Lutzer's claim that "there is some Saul in us all." Do you find that to be true in your own life?

2. What are some practical ways that we as Christians can avoid the spear throwers in our lives?

3. Read 1 Samuel 24:1–22. If David had killed Saul, would he have been justified in the act, or would he have committed a sin? Why?

4. Read 1 Samuel 26:6–21. At what point are we justified in taking action against someone who has wronged us?

5. Discuss the idea of waiting for God to right the wrongs we have suffered. What makes this so difficult?

6. Read 1 Corinthians 6:1–8. Is it ever appropriate for a Christian to sue another Christian in court? Is it ever appropriate for a Christian to sue a non-Christian?

7. Paul's statement in verse 7 is a difficult one: "To have lawsuits at all with one another is already a defeat for you. Why not rather suffer wrong? Why not rather be defrauded?" In your experience, what are the positive results of Christians allowing themselves to be wronged?

8. What practical steps should Christians take when they need to settle a major offense or wrongdoing?

GOING DEEPER

Read Matthew 18:15–35.

1. Summarize Jesus' method for confronting another Christian who has wronged you. Is this approach still applicable today?

2. Does Jesus' method in verses 15–17 apply when Christians have been wronged by non-Christians? Why or why not?

3. Discuss Jesus' words in verses 18–20. How should Christians today understand and apply these words?

4. Speaking practically, is there a limit to the forgiveness we should extend other Christians? What about non-Christians?

5. Summarize Jesus' parable in verses 23–35. How does it add to the prior conversation about responding to someone who has wronged you?

PERSONAL REFLECTION

The nation of Israel was a Roman territory in Jesus' day, which meant there were lots of Roman soldiers around. There was also an interesting law that required Roman subjects to walk with a soldier for a mile, carrying some of his gear and supplies, if he requested it.

That law sets the stage for Jesus' words in Matthew 5:41: "If anyone forces you to go one mile, go with him two miles." The immediate question is: Why would Jesus say that? Was He supporting the authority of the Roman law or Roman soldiers? Was this an advanced technique for evangelism or a missional lifestyle?

We can get an answer by exploring the broader context of the verse. Jesus said:

> You have heard that it was said, "An eye for an eye and a tooth for a tooth." But I say to you, Do not resist the one who is evil. But if anyone slaps you on the right cheek, turn to him the other also. And if anyone would sue you and take your tunic, let him have your cloak as well. And if anyone forces you to go one mile, go with him two miles. Give to the one who begs from you, and do not refuse the one who would borrow from you.

Those are hard words. Jesus isn't asking us to give up our desire for vengeance. He isn't advocating that we accept it when we experience a wrong. He's telling us to embrace it. He's commanding us to give up our rights in favor of discomfort, and even suffering.

Do you have the courage to obey?

Engaging the Topic answers:

1. dodge 2. evil 3. reason 4. spear thrower 5. God 6. lessons; teach

7. Jesus; evil

DVD Session Seven

WHEN BITTERNESS TAKES ROOT

In preparation for these discussion questions
and the DVD lecture, **please read:**
Chapter 7, "From Bitterness to Blessing"

From the Author

AS A FARM BOY growing up, one of my chores was to
weed the garden. I absolutely hated it. I had to put a stake in
the ground to distinguish between what was weeded and what
still needed to be weeded because I did the task so poorly!

But in the process I learned something valuable. There are
essentially two ways to take care of weeds: cut them off at
ground level or dig them out at the roots. Only the second
solves the problem.

When bitterness takes root in your life, it's nearly impossible to deal with it at the surface level. I've learned that our
choice to forgive might begin at a superficial level, but it must
continue to go deeper. At first the feelings of anger and pain

might go dormant for hours or days, but eventually, the bitterness raises its ugly head.

We need to attack bitterness at its root. That's what these final sessions are all about—root-level forgiveness and whenever possible, root-level reconciliation.

ENGAGING THE TOPIC

Answer these questions while watching the DVD and reading the book.

1. Bitterness has _____.

2. Bitterness _____.

3. Joseph, more than others, teaches us not only the lesson of _____ but _____ part in it all.

4. Joseph could have decided to be a _____, but he decided _____ would not define who he is.

5. Joseph had every right to be _____ against his _____.

6. The second reason Joseph had a right to be bitter was the _____ _____ made about him.

7. Joseph refused the temptation of Potiphar's wife because he had a right view of _____ and a right view of _____.

8. God does not allow _____ in our lives unless He intends it to do us some _____ and bear _____.

9. When your dream is being dashed to the ground, one of the best things you can do is to help somebody _____ his own _____.

OPENING ACTIVITY

Purpose: To help group members recognize bitterness.

Supplies: A small supply of bitter herbs and spices (e.g., cinnamon, horseradish, fenugreek, ground coffee, ginger, nutmeg, and so on). Arrange these on a tray with each in a small bowl before the group arrives.

Activity: To open the discussion, have group members describe specific foods they have eaten that involve a bitter taste. After they share their stories, give everyone a chance to experience bitterness as a flavor right now. Set out the tray and ask each participant to take a small taste from each bowl. When everyone has sampled the herbs and spices, allow a few moments for everyone to share their reactions:

- Why did you choose the herb or spice you tasted?
- How would you describe the flavor you experienced?
- Why do these herbs and spices have a valuable place in food preparation when they taste so bitter in isolation?

QUESTIONS FOR DISCUSSION

1. Discuss the metaphor of bitterness as an emotion with "roots." In what ways have you found that to be true?

2. In your experience, what are some common causes of bitterness in people today?

3. Read Genesis 37:1–4, 12–36. What specific emotions are described in this passage?

4. Which actions resulted in roots of bitterness being planted? In your opinion, who was at fault for this entire situation?

5. Read Genesis 39:7–23. What is the danger of giving in to sexual sin? What is the benefit of resisting temptation?

6. Is it true or false to say that God rewards those who choose to obey Him? Why do you say so?

7. Read Genesis 40:1–23. When have you experienced bitterness because of failed expectations?

8. How can you respond to a wrong in a way that prevents a root of bitterness from forming? What needs to change in you in order to allow such a response?

GOING DEEPER

Read Genesis 37:12–36.

1. Are Joseph's brothers the only ones to blame for this incident? If not, who else shares some of the responsibility?

2. Discuss Reuben's actions during this scene. Do you feel he behaved in a manner that was noble or cowardly? Why?

3. Discuss the significance of Joseph being sold to a caravan of Ishmaelites (see Genesis 21:8–21).

4. What are the most important lessons that Christians today can learn from this passage?

PERSONAL REFLECTION

Many lies, half-truths, and heresies have been connected with Christianity over the centuries. One of the most common (and most dangerous) is the idea that following God will inevitably lead to peace, comfort, and prosperity. This idea has grown deep roots in the lives of many Christians in today's culture.

Ironically, this deception often springs up when Christians misinterpret the pages of Scripture. People hear a verse like "For I know the plans I have for you, declares the Lord, plans for welfare and not for evil, to give you a future and a hope" (Jeremiah 29:11), and they believe that God's plan will lead them to well-being. But they forget that Jeremiah was writing to the Israelites living as captives in Babylon.

Jesus' own disciples were infected with this false belief. They believed their service to Him would result in earthly power and wealth. That's why they were so often confused by Jesus' references to His upcoming death.

After one of these references, Jesus spoke more clearly to His disciples, and they responded favorably: "Now you are speaking clearly and without figures of speech," they said. "Now we can see that you know all things and that you do not even need to have anyone ask you questions. This makes us believe that you came from God" (John 16:29–30).

Jesus' response seems half-sad, half-amused: "'Do you now believe?' Jesus replied. 'A time is coming and in fact has come when you will be scattered, each to your own home. You will leave me all alone. Yet I am not alone, for my Father is with me. I have told you these things, so that in me you may have peace. In this world you will have trouble. But take heart! I have overcome the world'" (verses 31–33).

That's the reality of following Jesus: He is in control, and yet "in this world you will have trouble." How will you respond?

Engaging the Topic answers:

1. roots 2. spreads 3. forgiveness; God's 4. victim; victimhood
5. bitter; brothers 6. false accusations 7. sin; God 8. injustice; good; fruit
9. fulfill; dream

WHEN YOU ARE READY TO LET GO

In preparation for these discussion questions
and the DVD lecture, **please read:**
Chapter 7, "From Bitterness to Blessing" (pages 122–31)
Chapter 9, "When Reconciliation Fails"

From the Author

I'M TOLD THAT when a rattlesnake is cornered it will sometimes bite itself. This self-inflicted punishment is perhaps done in anger or as a form of vengeance, but it hurts only the snake. Just so bitterness is a self-inflicted wound that hurts us but is of no concern to our enemy.

I don't know how to say it more strongly: we must let go of the bitterness and revenge that contaminates our souls. We are needlessly hurting ourselves.

Dear friend, if you are right now holding tighter to your bitterness from a wrong you've suffered than you are to this book, I urge you to lay down the book and surrender your pain to Christ. Only He is able to set you free from the prison of resentment. Don't allow the foolish, petty deeds of a long lost enemy chain you to a life of misery and anger. Your marriage has suffered long enough; your children have endured the brunt of your angry outbursts for too long already; your ministry is dangling by a very thin thread. Give it up now. Let your wounds become scars and start living again.

Will you do that today? I pray that you will.

ENGAGING THE TOPIC

Answer these questions while watching the DVD and reading the book.

1. Joseph chose to live in the _____, not the _____.

2. God is bigger than all the _____.

3. Joseph chose to _____ his brothers _____.

4. Joseph saw _____ in the injustice.

5. The act of the brothers' sin itself must be seen as part of God's _____.

6. Joseph _____ his brothers rather than _____ his brothers.

7. Joseph refused to _____.

8. _____ does not heal family feuds.

9. Bitterness is contrary to _____.

OPENING ACTIVITY

Purpose: To help group members glimpse the futility of refusing to let go.

Supplies: One large ice cube for group member; paper towels.

Activity: Gather all the group members into a circle and give each person a large ice cube. Instruct everyone to close their hand firmly around it so that they are squeezing the cube in their fists. As soon as everyone has their ice cubes in their fists, explain that this is a contest to see who can hold on to an ice cube the longest. Go!

At first the cold will become uncomfortable. Then it will become mildly painful. Finally, people will begin dropping their ice cubes. (Make sure you have paper towels handy to clean up the melted water.) When the last person is still holding an ice cube (or when everyone has dropped out), announce the contest over. Then discuss the following questions to unpack the experience:

- What did it feel like to clutch an ice cube?
- What motivated you to keep holding as the pain increased?
- What benefit came to the winner after holding on the longest?
- What advantages came with letting go?

QUESTIONS FOR DISCUSSION

1. What are the benefits of holding on to bitterness and pain? Why do people choose to hold on to their bitterness and pain?

2. Read Genesis 45:1–15. Have you ever been in a position to punish someone for a wrong they committed against you? What emotions did you experience in that moment?

3. Discuss Joseph's claim in verse 8 that "it was not you who sent me here, but God." Does that mean Joseph's brothers were not culpable for their actions? Why?

4. In chapter 7 of the book, Dr. Lutzer asserts that we can only move beyond our past when we can embrace it as part of God's plan. How do you react to this statement?

5. Read Genesis 50:15–21. What insight does this provide into the mind-set of Joseph's brothers?

6. Describe the ways that Joseph's words, actions, and attitudes are countercultural for today's society.

7. Chapter 9 describes a phenomenon called "one-sided forgiveness." What is the value of this type of forgiveness? Why is it necessary for the process of letting go?

8. If you are willing, share the deep areas of bitterness and pain that you are still holding tightly. What needs to happen for you to let go?

GOING DEEPER

Read Romans 12:9–21.

1. Which of these commands stands out to you most strongly? Why is that?

2. Do any of these commands seem unrealistic to expect of Christians today? Do any seem unrealistic to expect of you?

3. Do you find it easy or hard to "bless those who persecute you"? Has this changed throughout the course of your life?

4. Summarize the commands in verses 14–20 on how to respond when you've been wronged. Are you able to respond this way?

5. What would it look like to be "overcome by evil"? What steps will you need to take in order to "overcome evil with good"?

Personal Reflection

In Genesis 41:50–52 there is an interesting sidebar to Joseph's story:

Before the year of famine came, two sons were born to Joseph. Asenath, the daughter of Potiphera priest of On, bore them to him. Joseph called the name of the firstborn Manasseh. "For," he said, "God has made me forget all my hardship and all my father's house." The name of the second he called Ephraim, "For God has made me fruitful in the land of my affliction."

It's worth noticing the progression present in the names Joseph chooses for his sons. First is Manasseh, because "God has made me forget all my hardship and all my father's house."

The ability to forget can be a blessing, and that was the case for Joseph after all that he had suffered. His second son is Ephraim, because "God has made me fruitful in the land of my affliction." Joseph's experiences went well beyond finding a silver lining on a cloudy day. He experienced God's favor in a deep and full measure—eventually.

The question that needs to be asked is: Could there have been an Ephraim without a Manasseh? In other words, was it necessary for Joseph to forget his past—to let go of the wrongs he had suffered and move on—before he could experience the full and fruitful life God desired for him?

We can't know the answer for sure when it comes to Joseph, but the general principle is a good one. If you have been wronged, or even if you are in the process of being wronged, you can still live a life that is full and fruitful under the blessing of God—but first there are some decisions you need to make. Stop. Surrender. Forgive. Let go. Move on.

What do you say?

Engaging the Topic answers:
1. future; past 2. if-onlys 3. set; free 4. God 5. providence
6. blessed; curse 7. retaliate 8. Time 9. faith